CHECKERBOARD BIOGRAPHIES

TAYLOR SWIFT

ELSIE OLSON

Checkerboard
Library

An Imprint of Abdo Publishing
abdobooks.com

ABDOBOOKS.COM

Published by Abdo Publishing, a division of ABDO, PO Box 398166, Minneapolis, Minnesota 55439.
Copyright © 2022 by Abdo Consulting Group, Inc. International copyrights reserved in all countries.
No part of this book may be reproduced in any form without written permission from the publisher.
Checkerboard Library™ is a trademark and logo of Abdo Publishing.

Printed in the United States of America, North Mankato, Minnesota
052021
092021

THIS BOOK CONTAINS RECYCLED MATERIALS

Design and Production: Mighty Media, Inc.
Editor: Liz Salzmann
Cover Photograph: Jordan Strauss/AP/Shutterstock Images
Interior Photographs: Andrew Orth © 2004, p. 7; DFree/Shutterstock Images, p. 19; Everett Collection/
    Shutterstock Images, p. 13; Featureflash Photo Agency/Shutterstock Images, p. 15; Jordan Strauss/AP
    Images, p. 27; Kathy Hutchins/Shutterstock Images, pp. 23, 29 (bottom right); KGC-49/STAR MAX/IPx/
    AP Images, p. 25; Liam Goodner/Shutterstock Images, pp. 5, 28 (bottom); Michael Hicks/Wikimedia
    Commons, pp. 21, 29; Press Line Photos/Shutterstock Images, pp. 17, 29 (top); s_bukley/Shutterstock
    Images, pp. 9, 11, 28; Shutterstock Images, p. 19 (paper clip)

Library of Congress Control Number: 2021933242

Publisher's Cataloging-in-Publication Data
Names: Olson, Elsie, author.
Title: Taylor Swift / by Elsie Olson
Description: Minneapolis, Minnesota : Abdo Publishing, 2022 | Series: Checkerboard biographies | Includes
    online resources and index.
Identifiers: ISBN 9781532196034 (lib. bdg.) | ISBN 9781098216894 (ebook)
Subjects: LCSH: Swift, Taylor, -- 1989- --Juvenile literature. | Singers--United States--Biography--Juvenile
    literature. | Women country musicians--United States--Biography--Juvenile literature. | Actors and
    actresses--Biography--Juvenile literature. | Women rock musicians--United States--Biography--Juvenile
    literature. | Businesspeople--Biography--Juvenile literature.
Classification: DDC 781.642--dc23

CONTENTS

CHAPTER 1

SONGWRITING SUPERSTAR

Taylor Swift is a famous singer-songwriter. She started writing music when she was just 12 years old. Swift started out as a country music artist. But today, she is one of the world's biggest pop stars.

Swift has sold more than 40 million records. This makes her one of the best-selling artists of all time. Swift writes or cowrites every song on her albums. Her songs often draw from her own life and experiences. Swift is also famous for finding ways to connect with her fans on social media and in real life.

In addition to being a pop star, Swift is a **feminist** and an **activist**. She uses her celebrity to speak about issues including women's rights and gun control. Swift is more than just a musician. She is a role model for young women around the world.

Five of Swift's albums have been the best-selling albums of the year.

CHAPTER 2

THE ROAD TO NASHVILLE

Taylor Alison Swift was born on December 13, 1989, in West Reading, Pennsylvania. Her father, Scott, worked as a **stockbroker**. Her mother, Andrea, stayed home, raising Taylor and Taylor's younger brother, Austin.

By the time she was ten, Taylor was performing at local talent shows. When she was 11, she sang the national **anthem** at a Philadelphia 76ers basketball game. At age 12, Taylor started taking guitar lessons. She also wrote her first song, "Lucky You."

Taylor attended Wyomissing Area Junior/Senior High School. But she dreamed of being a country music star. Nashville, Tennessee is the center of the country music world. So, Taylor's parents began taking her on frequent trips to Nashville.

When she was 14, Taylor signed a deal with Nashville record company Sony/ATV to be a songwriter. The Swift family moved to nearby Hendersonville, Tennessee. There, Taylor continued chasing her dream.

Music was an important part of Taylor's life from a young age. She was named after folk-rock singer James Taylor. And her grandmother, Marjorie Finlay, was an opera singer.

CHAPTER 3

SONGWRITER EXTRAORDINAIRE

In 2004, Taylor performed at Nashville's Bluebird Cafe. The cafe held performances that featured new songwriters. Record executive Scott Borchetta saw Taylor's performance. Afterward, he told Taylor he was starting a record label, Big Machine Records. In 2006, Taylor became one of Big Machine's first artists.

Taylor soon got to work on her first album. Every song on the album was written or cowritten by Taylor. This was unusual. Most country artists performed songs written by other people. Taylor often worked with songwriter Liz Rose. Taylor would come up with ideas for songs, and Rose helped her develop them.

Taylor based her songs on her own life and relationships. Her first single, "Tim McGraw," was released to radio stations in June 2006. The song was based on a high school boyfriend. Taylor had gotten the idea for the song while sitting in math class.

Swift with country singer Tim McGraw. In 2013, she worked with McGraw on the song "Highway Don't Care."

On October 24, Taylor released her first full-length album, *Taylor Swift*. It sold 40,000 copies in its first week. Within a year, it had sold more than 1 million copies! Music critics loved the album. Although the album was country, many songs had a pop music feel. This gave the album a wider appeal.

Taylor went on tour to promote the album. On tour, she was the opening act for other country artists. Taylor had been attending traditional high school. But she couldn't go while on tour. So, Taylor **enrolled** in a homeschool program. This allowed Taylor to finish high school while touring. She graduated in 2008.

Meanwhile, Taylor had been working on her next album, *Fearless*. As on her first album, Taylor wrote or cowrote every song. She was also one of the album's **producers**.

Taylor released *Fearless* on November 11, 2008. The album sold more than 500,000 copies in its first week. It became the best-selling album of 2009 and earned Taylor her first Grammy Awards.

Fearless won Grammy Awards for both Album of the Year and Country Album of the Year. The song "White Horse" won Best Country Song and Best Female Country Vocal Performance.

CHAPTER 4

SWIFT INTERRUPTED

Swift finished her *Fearless* tour in the summer of 2010. It was a huge success. Most of the shows had sold out. During the tour, Swift performed alongside famous musicians, including John Mayer and Katy Perry. Swift had also designed the tour sets herself.

On September 13, 2009, Swift attended the MTV Video Music Awards (VMAs). Swift won the award for Best Female Music Video for her song "You Belong with Me." As she was accepting her award, rapper Kanye West rushed onstage. He took the microphone and told the **audience** that singer Beyoncé should have won. Both Swift and Beyoncé were shocked and embarrassed. The incident made headlines around the world.

The incident helped keep Swift's name in the news. It also served as inspiration for her next album. On October 25, 2010, Swift released *Speak Now*. The song "Innocent" was written about West.

Swift's *Fearless* tour was praised for its costumes and theatrics.

Speak Now earned mostly positive reviews. Critics praised Swift's songwriting. Fans loved the album too. It sold more than 1 million copies in its first week!

The album's songs were very personal to Swift. For the past few years, Swift had had several high-profile relationships with other celebrities. Her fans loved trying to figure out which celebrities the songs could be about.

Swift spent 2011 and early 2012 touring and promoting *Speak Now*. During that time, she also wrote and recorded her next album. On October 22, 2012, Swift released *Red*. The album had more of a pop music sound than her past albums. *Red* sold more than 1 million copies in its first week. Swift promoted the album with a tour during 2013 and 2014.

SWIFTIES

Swift values her relationship with her fans, known as Swifties. She connects with them on social media. She sends them surprise gifts, handwritten notes, and home-baked cookies. She has even invited fans to her home. She has also helped fans pay bills, such as student loans or medical bills.

Swift is known for her willingness to meet and take photos with her fans.

CHAPTER 5

GOING POP

In 2014, Swift moved from Nashville to New York City. On October 27, she released the album *1989*. Its first song was "Welcome to New York."

The album marked a turning point in Swift's career. Her past albums had all been marketed as country albums, even as she embraced a more pop sound. But *1989* was a **synth-pop** album inspired by pop music from the 1980s. Swift still wrote or cowrote every song on the album. But she worked with some new writers and **producers**, including well-known pop producer Jack Antonoff.

Like her previous two albums, *1989* sold more than 1 million copies its first week. Most critics loved Swift's new sound, giving the album good reviews. And Swift won three Grammy Awards for the album, including Album of the Year. This made Swift the first female solo artist to win Album of the Year twice.

CAT LADY

Swift has described herself as a cat lady. She has three pet cats that she posts about regularly on social media.

Swift was often photographed with celebrity friends, known as "the Squad." *Left to right*: Gigi Hadid, Martha Hunt, Hailee Steinfeld, Cara Delevingne, Selena Gomez, Swift, Serayah, Lily Aldridge

CHAPTER 6

STREAMING WARS

Swift had become one of the biggest music stars in the world. But the industry was changing. More and more listeners were listening to streaming services, such as Spotify. This led to lower album sales.

Swift felt the streaming companies weren't paying artists enough for their songs. In November 2014, Swift pulled her entire collection of music from Spotify.

In 2015, Swift faced off with another industry giant, Apple Music. That June, Apple announced it would be offering free trials of its new streaming service. However, it would not be paying artists for any music streamed during that time. Swift felt this policy was unfair. She posted on social media site Tumblr about her disappointment. Soon after, Apple announced it was changing its policy.

Swift eventually made peace with Spotify. In 2017, she announced she was releasing her full collection on the streaming service. Spotify had changed its music licensing policy to better support artists. And streaming had become more popular than ever.

BIO BASICS

NAME: Taylor Swift

NICKNAME: Tay Tay

BIRTH: December 13, 1989, West Reading, Pennsylvania

FAMOUS FOR: singing, songwriting, and performing

ACHIEVEMENTS: wrote or cowrote songs on nine studio albums; appeared in several films and TV shows; first female solo artist to win the Grammy for Album of the Year twice (2010 and 2016) and then a third time (2021).

> " Music is art, and art is important and rare. Important, rare things are valuable. Valuable things should be paid for. It's my opinion that music should not be free. "

CHAPTER 7

BAD REPUTATION

The years following *1989*'s release proved to be challenging for Swift. In 2015, her mother was **diagnosed** with **cancer**. Swift had also become a frequent target in magazine articles. People criticized her dating life. She had public **feuds** with other high-profile celebrities, including Katy Perry and Kanye West.

Swift had spent most of her career controlling what the media said about her. Now, it seemed the entire internet had turned against Swift. She responded by taking a break from the spotlight, saying, "I think people might need a break from me."

For most of 2017, Swift stopped posting on social media. But she didn't stop writing and recording songs. On November 6, 2017, she released her next album, *Reputation*.

Reputation's sound was much different from her past albums. It was influenced by R&B, pop, hip-hop, and electronic music. It didn't sell as well as her previous albums. But the album received good reviews from critics. Some called it her best album yet.

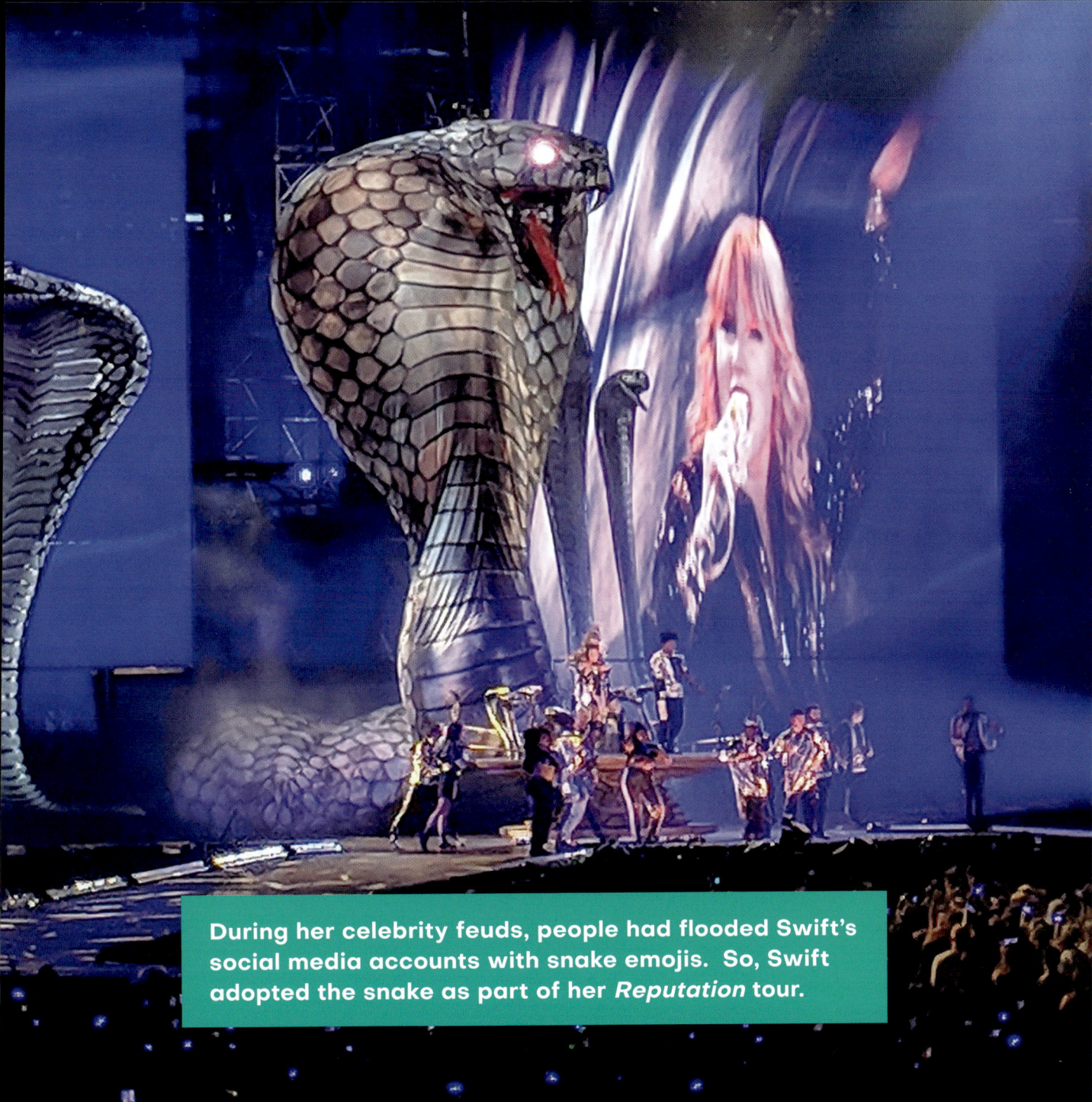

During her celebrity feuds, people had flooded Swift's social media accounts with snake emojis. So, Swift adopted the snake as part of her *Reputation* tour.

CHAPTER 8

POLITICS & A NEW LABEL

While working on *Reputation*, Swift had also been filming a documentary about her life. The film, *Miss Americana*, was released in January 2020. The film gave viewers an up-close look into Swift's life.

In the documentary, Swift talks about her struggles with fame and life in the spotlight. Viewers can see her process as she writes and records songs. Swift also discusses her decision to start speaking out on social and political issues.

For most of her career, Swift had tried to stay out of politics. She hoped to avoid commenting on topics that could affect ticket and album sales. But in 2018, Swift publicly supported Democratic candidates running for Congress in her home state of Tennessee.

Swift also encouraged fans to vote. This led to a rise in voter registration. Swift also spoke out in favor of gun control and against **sexism**. For many, Swift was becoming a **feminist** icon.

In *Miss Americana*, Swift discusses how sharing political views can alienate some fans.

On August 23, 2019, Swift released her seventh studio album, *Lover*. The album was lighter and happier than *Reputation*. It centered heavily around her relationship with actor Joe Alwyn, whom Swift had been dating since 2017. The album received good reviews and sold well.

Lover was Swift's first album with a new label. In 2018, she had signed with Republic Records. Under her new contract, Swift would own all her masters. These are the original song recordings. However, this only applied to new recordings. Swift's original masters still belonged to Big Machine.

In 2019, music agent Scooter Braun bought Big Machine's entire catalog, including Swift's masters. Swift was angry with Borchetta for not giving her the chance to buy her masters before the sale.

Soon after the sale, Swift announced that she would rerecord the albums now owned by Braun. Then she would have new masters of her songs. She felt this was a way to regain control of her music.

FILMS & TV

In 2019, Swift was in the movie *Cats*. The film received poor reviews. But critics praised Swift's performance. *Cats* was not Swift's first acting role. She also appeared in *The Giver*, *The Lorax*, and *Valentine's Day*. Swift also appeared in several TV shows.

Swift and Alwyn kept their relationship private by rarely being photographed together.

CHAPTER 9

SWEET SURPRISES

In 2020, the COVID-19 pandemic stopped most live performances. So, Swift spent the summer at home with Alwyn writing and recording music. On July 24, Swift released a surprise album, *Folklore*.

Folklore was completely different from Swift's past albums. She worked remotely with well-known folk and indie rock musicians. This gave the album a mellow and dreamy tone. Swift surprised the world again when she released another album, *Evermore*, on December 11. Swift described *Evermore* as a sister album to *Folklore*.

In February 2021, Swift announced she had finished rerecording her 2008 album *Fearless*. She released the first single "Love Story: Taylor's Version," on February 12. The full album was released in April. The new *Fearless* included six new songs that had been cut from the original album.

Through all the ups and downs in her career, Swift never wavered in her devotion to her music or her fans. As she once said, "People haven't always been there for me, but music always has."

In 2021, *Folklore* became Swift's third album to win the Grammy for Album of the Year. This made Swift the first woman to win Album of the Year three times.

TIMELINE

1989
Taylor Alison Swift is born on December 13, in West Reading, Pennsylvania.

2008
Taylor graduates from high school. She releases *Fearless* on November 11.

2012
Swift releases *Red* on October 22.

2006
Taylor signs with Scott Borchetta's Big Machine record label. She releases her album, *Taylor Swift*, on October 24.

2010
Swift releases *Speak Now* on October 25.

2014

Swift releases *1989* on October 27. The album marks her transition to pop music and goes on to win three Grammys.

2019

Swift releases *Lover* on August 23.

2021

Swift releases her first rerecorded album, *Fearless*.

2017

Swift releases *Reputation* on November 6.

2020

Swift stars in the documentary *Miss Americana*. She releases surprise sister albums *Folklore* on July 24 and *Evermore* on December 11.

GLOSSARY

activist—a person who takes direct action in support of or in opposition to an issue that causes disagreement.

anthem—a song of gladness or patriotism.

audience—a group of people watching a performance.

cancer—any of a group of often deadly diseases marked by harmful changes in the normal growth of cells. Cancer can spread and destroy healthy tissues and organs.

COVID-19—a serious illness that first appeared in late 2019.

diagnose—to recognize something, such as a disease, by signs, symptoms, or tests.

documentary—a film that artistically presents facts, often about an event or a person.

enroll—to register, especially in order to attend a school.

feminist—one who believes that women and men should have equal rights and opportunities.

feud—a long, bitter fight or disagreement between two people, families, or groups.

pandemic—an outbreak of a disease that spreads quickly throughout the world.

producer—a person who oversees or provides money for a play, TV show, movie, or album.

sexism—unfair treatment of someone because of his or her sex.

stockbroker—a person that handles orders to buy and sell stocks. Stocks are the shares or portions into which a company or a business is divided.

synth-pop—short for "synthesizer pop," a type of pop music in which the synthesizer is the main instrument.

ONLINE RESOURCES

To learn more about Taylor Swift, please visit **abdobooklinks.com** or scan this QR code. These links are routinely monitored and updated to provide the most current information available.

INDEX